# The Best Slow Cooker Lunch Recipes

*Easy and Tasty Recipes for Slow Cooker*

Porzia Schneider

Sommario

**Lunch Recipes**............................................................7

**French Onion Soup for Slow Cooker**........................7

**Maple Bacon and White Bean Soup**.......................9

**Chicken Minestrone in Slow Cooker**....................12

**Tomato Soup with Rigatoni**..................................14

**Chicken and Burrito Bowls**...................................16

**Mac and Cheese pasta in Slow Cooker**.................19

**Pumpkin couscous with lamb**..............................21

**Pappardelle ragout with duck**.............................24

**Oxtail and Chorizo Stew**......................................27

**Slow Cooker Soup with Ham**................................29

**Slow Cooker Soup with Celery and Bacon**...........31

**Lamb Shank in Slow Cooker**.................................34

**Spicy chicken with fennel stew**...........................36

**French Farmhouse Chicken Soup**.........................38

**Bean soup served with toasts**.............................40

**Chicken ragout with red wine**.............................43

**Egg noodles with Red Beef**..................................46

**Autumn Pumpkin Soup**........................................49

**Bone Broth in Slow Cooker**..................................51

**Creamy vegetable curry with chickpea**................53

**Lamb Chunks with Honey**.....................................55

**Chickpea curry with vegetables**..........................58

**Soup with lentils and goat cheese**......................60

**Ragout with Beef and Carrot**...............................63

**Ham and pea soup foe Slow Cooker**............................ 65

**Summer Curry in Slow Cooker** ............................... 67

**Slow Cooker meatballs with rigatoni** ....................... 70

Cucumber Salad in Jar ............................................. 72

Brie Cheese in Pastry .............................................. 74

Pulled Beef ........................................................... 75

Mushroom and Cheese Sandwich ............................... 77

Beans Pasta Bolognese ............................................ 79

Lettuce Chicken Salad ............................................ 81

Spaghetti Bolognese ............................................... 83

Paprika Soup ........................................................ 85

Lunch Cream Soup ................................................. 87

Chicken Salad ...................................................... 89

Spicy Red Soup .................................................... 91

Cheddar Soup ...................................................... 93

Oregano Rolls ...................................................... 95

Coconut Spinach Casserole ...................................... 97

Stuffed Meatloaf................................................... 99

Lunch Schnitzel....................................................101

Stuffed Mozzarella Caprese ....................................103

Veggie and Beef Lasagna.........................................105

Meat Taco...........................................................107

Fresh Cottage Cheese .............. Errore. Il segnalibro non è definito.

Lunch Tortillas....................... Errore. Il segnalibro non è definito.

Mushroom and Cream Bowl . Errore. Il segnalibro non è definito.

Keto Pizza .................................. Errore. Il segnalibro non è definito.

# INTRODUCTION

Hello there! Invite to my book of recipes for the Crock Pot. My dishes are simply also scrumptious to maintain to myself. As well as it's the only cookbook you'll require to make one of the most delicious Crockery Pot recipes you have actually ever tasted!

If there's one cooking area device I can't live without, it's my Crockery Pot. This device has changed my life totally in the kitchen area! Gone are the days when I invested hours each week, prepping and after that cooking meals. And so many times those meals were tasteless, with leftovers that no one intended to consume.

Then along came my Crock Pot Pressure Cooker ... and also now I make scrumptious dishes daily.

One of the greatest enticing features of the Crock Pot is that it makes fresh and also quick cozy dishes quickly. Whether you're vegan or love your meat as well as hen, my publication has the best recipes for making fantastic, healthier meals. And also ensure you make a lavish rip off recipe on those days when you're not counting calories and also fat! Those are the most effective dishes of all. In this publication, I share my favorite.

## French Onion Soup for Slow Cooker

Perfect choice for French cuisine fans!

**Prep time: 30 minutes Cooking time: 12 hours Servings: 6**

INGREDIENTS:

3 yellow onions

2 tbsp. olive oil

2 tbsp. melted butter (unsalted)

Black pepper (freshly ground)

Pinch salt

10 cups beef broth

2 tbsp. balsamic vinegar

3 tbsp. brandy (optional)

6 baguette slices (to serve)

2 cups Gruyere cheese (to serve)

**Chopped shallot or onion**

## DIRECTIONS:

Chop the onion and place it into large Slow Cooker. Mix in the butter, salt, olive oil and black pepper. Cook on low overnight.

In the morning, add to onion the broth and balsamic vinegar.

Cover with the lid and cook for another 6-8 hours on LOW (the longer you cook, the more intensively flavors you will get).

Pour the soup into small bowls and place them into preheated oven. Top each bowl with the toast and cheese and bake for 30 minutes.

To serve, place the chopped onions on a side of each bowl.

**Nutrition: Calories: 455 Fat: 33g Carbohydrates: 61g Protein: 54g**

## Maple Bacon and White Bean Soup

Try this soup with bacon – and it will be your favorite!

**Prep time: 25 minutes Cooking time: 12 hours Servings: 8**

INGREDIENTS:

**Two cups white beans (dried)**

**One red pepper**

**1 ham bone**

**8 cups chicken broth**

**5 slices maple bacon**

**2 carrots**

**1 red pepper**

**1 onion**

**Half cup diced ham**

**2 celery stalks**

**Thyme**

**4 cloves garlic**

**Zest and juice of half lemon**

**Salt and pepper to taste**

**Chopped parsley (fresh)**

DIRECTIONS:

In a deep bowl, cover the beans with cold water and leave to soak overnight.

In the morning drain the beans and place them into Slow Cooker, cover with broth and add ham. Cook on high for 3-4 hours.

In a small frying pan, cook the bacon slices until crispy. Add the red pepper, onion, celery, garlic and carrots. Add salt and cook for ten minutes

Add the aromatic mixture into Slow Cooker and stir well with beans.

Let cook on HIGH for an hour or two. In the end, add the chopped parsley and lemon zest. You can serve it hot or cold – it is tasty both ways.

**Nutrition: Calories: 443 Fat: 32g Carbohydrates: 65g
Protein: 33g**

## Chicken Minestrone in Slow Cooker

Easy to make and very delicious!

**Prep time: 5 minutes Cooking time: 3 hours Servings: 3**

INGREDIENTS:

**2 chicken thighs**

**1 bay leaf**

**One medium leek**

**1 can tomatoes**

**Three cloves garlic**

**3 medium carrots**

**One teaspoon salt**

**2 celery stalks**

**4 cups chicken broth**

**2 cups water**

**4 cups shredded cabbage**

**1 can beans**

**One medium zucchini**

**DIRECTIONS:**

To make the broth, preheat Slow Cooker and place in it the chicken, leek, tomatoes with juice, celery, bay leaf, carrots, garlic. Add some pepper and salt to taste.

Cover with water and chicken broth and cook for 6 hours on low mode. Cut the chard leaves into one-inch pieces and place in separate bowl.

Add the sliced cabbage, halved zucchini and refrigerate until the broth is prepared.

When the broth is ready, add in the vegetable and combine well. Turn the Slow Cooker on HIGH and leave for 30 minutes.

To serve, add the pasta into your soup.

**Nutrition: Calories: 551 Fat: 37g Carbohydrates: 42g Protein: 53g**

# Tomato Soup with Rigatoni

You should try this Italian receipt!

**Prep time: 25 minutes Cooking time: 3 hours Servings: 8**

## INGREDIENTS:

**6 cups tomato sauce**

**2 tbsp. olive oil**

**Salt**

**Half tsp sugar**

**One package rigatoni**

**4 cloves garlic**

**2cups whole-milk**

**Half cup Parmesan Cheese**

**Red pepper to taste**

## DIRECTIONS:

Coat the inside dish of your Slow Cooker with a cooking spray Rinse the rigatoni in cold water and drain carefully.

Right in the bowl of your Slow Cooker mix the noodles, cottage cheese, tomato sauce, one cup shredded mozzarella, olive oil, spinach, garlic, sugar, red pepper and salt. Stir well.

Turn on the Slow Cooker and set the LOW temperature mode. Prepare the rigatoni for 3-4 hours. In ten minutes before ready cover with Parmesan and cook until the cheese is melted.

**Nutrition: Calories: 469 Fat: 43g Carbohydrates: 55g Protein: 63g**

# Chicken and Burrito Bowls

Small bowl and plenty of energy!

**Prep time: 5 minutes Cooking time: 3 hours Servings: 3**

INGREDIENTS:

**One or two chicken breasts (boneless)**

**2 tsp chili powder**

**One cup brown rice**

**2 tsp salt**

**One cup chicken stock**

**One can diced tomatoes**

**One teaspoon cumin**

**One cup frozen corn**

**One can black beans**

## DIRECTIONS:

Cover the chicken breasts with diced tomatoes, mix well and add half-cup chicken stock, cumin, chili powder and salt.

Place in a wide Slow Cooker dish. Ingredients should cover chicken evenly. Cover the lid and leave the chicken to cook on HIGH for 3-4 hours.

When it is time, add the rice, frozen corn, black beans and chicken corn. Continue to cook under the lid for another 4 hours.

When the rice is ready, use two forks and shred the chicken into small pieces (bite-size). Serve the burrito in small bowls garnished with cheese or diced green onions.

**Nutrition: Calories: 551 Fat: 30g Carbohydrates: 146g Protein: 51g**

## Mac and Cheese pasta in Slow Cooker

Amazing pasta for your healthy lunch!

**Prep time: 26 minutes Cooking time: 2-3 hours Servings: 8**

INGREDIENTS:

**3 cups shredded Cheddar**

**Half teaspoon salt**

**Two cups whole milk**

**One cap elbow macaroni**

**Half teaspoon dry mustard**

**Two cups whole milk**

DIRECTIONS:

Combine the ingredients (except cheese) in Slow Cooker. Stir well to combine everything evenly. Cover with the lid and cook on HIGH from 2 to 4 hours.

In 2 hours after you started the cooking process, check if the pasta is soft and there is no liquid. When it is 10 minutes remaining to finish, sprinkle the cheese over the pasta and cook until the cheese is melted.

Serve this pasta straight from the cooking dish.

**Nutrition: Calories: 566 Fat: 36g Carbohydrates: 48g Protein: 61g**

## Pumpkin couscous with lamb

Perfect for autumn!

**Prep time: 10 minutes Cooking time: 2-3 hours Servings: 6**

INGREDIENTS:

**2 tbsp. olive oil**

**Two red onions (halved and sliced)**

**2 cinnamon sticks**

**6 lamb shanks**

**3 garlic cloves**

**3tsp cumin (ground)**

**2 tsp paprika**

**4cups Massel beef stock**

**Cherry tomatoes (canned)**

**Half cup chopped coriander (fresh)**

**2 tbsp. brown sugar**

**Butternut pumpkin**

**2 cups couscous**

**Half cup fresh mint (chopped)**

DIRECTIONS:

Heat your Slow Cooker to 180 degrees.

Cover the frying skillet with 1-tablespoon olive oil and cook the lamb for 5-7 minutes (until brown). Transfer to the Slow Cooker dish.

Using the remaining oil, fry the onion until soft. Add cumin, crushed garlic, cinnamon, paprika and coriander. Leave for a minute until aromatic.

Add sugar, tomato, half the mint and half the fresh coriander. Stir in the beef stock. Pour the mixture into Slow Cooker.

Cook for 3-4 hours on HIGH temperature mode.

To serve, divide among bowls and garnish with remaining mint and coriander.

**Nutrition: Calories: 480 Fat: 14g Carbohydrates: 31g Protein: 32g**

## Pappardelle ragout with duck

Hot ragout for lunch – what else do you need for a beautiful day?

**Prep time: 30 minutes Cooking time: 4-5 hours Servings: 6**

**INGREDIENTS:**

**One small onion (brown and chopped)**

**Frozen duck**

**Half cup pancetta**

**One celery stick**

**Two garlic cloves**

**One carrot (small)**

**2 bay leaves (dried)**

**Three rosemary sprigs**

**One cup chicken stock**

**One cup pinot noir**

**Half cup green olives**

**Pappardelle pasta (to serve)**

**Parmesan (finely grated, to serve)**

**Chopped parsley (to serve)**

DIRECTIONS:

Prepare the duck: discard backbone and take off all exec fat. Quarter the duck and cover with salt. Cook the duck in a deep buttered skillet over high heat until it gets brown (for 5-6 minutes).

Preheat your Slow Cooker to 110 degrees. Cover the dish with reserved chicken fat.

In a separate pan, cook the onion, pancetta, carrot, celery, bay leaves and garlic. Stir time after time.

Place duck and vegetable mixture into Slow Cooker. Cover with wine, tomato and stock. Add rosemary.

Cover the lid and cook on high mode for 4 hours. Serve with parmesan, pasta and parsley.

**Nutrition: Calories: 504 Fat: 23g Carbohydrates: 7g Protein: 51g**

# Oxtail and Chorizo Stew

This is easier than you think! Just let it try and cook this!

**Prep time: 25 minutes Cooking time: 4 hours Servings: 4**

INGREDIENTS:

**Oxtail pieces**

**4 tbsp olive oil (extra virgin)**

**1 garlic cloves**

**1 onion (chopped)**

**1 tsp paprika**

**1 primo chorizo**

**1carrot (chopped)**

**Half orange zest**

**2rosemary sprigs**

**2 cans tomatoes (whole peeled)**

**2 cups red wine**

**14-16 cherry tomatoes**

**Flat-leaf parsley (to garnish)**

**3 cups beef stock**

DIRECTIONS:

Preheat your Slow Cooker to 170 degrees and butter the dish.

Place oxtail to a large saucepan and cover with cold water. Slowly bring to the boil and prepare for 15-20 minutes. Rinse and set aside.

Preheat olive oil in a large saucepan. Add onion, carrot, chorizo and garlic. Stir and cook for 4 minutes.

Add paprika, 1 rosemary sprig and orange zest. Salt and pepper.

Place oxtails in the Slow Cooker dish, cover with vegetables and tomato. Pour in wine and stock. Cook for 3-4 hours on high.

Serve with mash potatoes or any other side dish you like.

**Nutrition: Calories: 544 Fat: 39g Carbohydrates: 49g Protein: 33g**

## Slow Cooker Soup with Ham

Delicious and healthy soup for your middle day!

**Prep time: 23 minutes Cooking time: 8 hours Servings: 8**

INGREDIENTS:

**2 cups navy beans**

**2 large carrots**

**6 large potatoes**

**2 medium shallots**

**2 large celery stalks**

**1 ham bone**

**Salt**

**8 cups water**

**Thyme leaves**

**Minced sage**

**1 loaf crusty bread**

## DIRECTIONS:

In a large plate, stir the potatoes, celery, beans, carrots, shallots sage and thyme. You can do it right in Slow Cooker, but then do not forget to butter it.

Place the vegetable mix into Slow Cooker and nestle the ham bone in the middle. Pour in the water to cover evenly all the ingredients.

Cover with the lid and cook on LOW regime for 8 hours.

Remove ham bone, cool and shred it, then combine again with the soup. Serve hot with crusty baguette.

**Nutrition: Calories: 467 Fat: 28g Carbohydrates: 43g Protein: 52g**

# Slow Cooker Soup with Celery and Bacon

Try to cook it overnight – and you will get a perfect dish the next day!

**Prep time: 27 minutes Cooking time: 7 hours Servings: 4-6**

INGREDIENTS:

**One yellow onion (large)**

**10-12 small white potatoes**

**One bunch celery**

**3garlic cloves**

**4cups chicken broth**

**6-4 slices bacon (thick-cut)**

**Salt**

**Half teaspoon white pepper**

**4 tbsp heavy cream or milk**

## DIRECTIONS:

Preheat your Slow Cooker for 100-110 degrees and butter the cooking dish.

Chop the celery, potatoes and onion into medium and equally sized cubes. Mince the garlic. Place the prepared vegetables in your Slow Cooker and cover with chicken broth.

Season with pepper and salt to taste. Cook on LOW mode for 5-7 hours.

Before serving, puree the soup with a stick blender (can do iy right in Slow Cooker) and serve in small bowls with bacon over top.

**Nutrition: Calories: 577 Fat: 43g Carbohydrates: 46g Protein: 33g**

## Lamb Shank in Slow Cooker

Try this lamb – and you will not forget it!

**Prep time: 15 minutes Cooking time: 3 hours Servings: 6**

INGREDIENTS:

**2 tbsp. plain flour**

**2 tbsp. olive oil**

**Six lamb shanks**

**One brown onion**

**Half cup red wine**

**2 cups tomato pasta**

**2 garlic cloves**

**2 cups chicken broth or stock**

**3 sprigs rosemary (fresh)**

**5 small potatoes**

**One peeled turnip**

**chopped fresh parsley**

DIRECTIONS:

Mix the flour with salt and pepper. Place the lamb shanks into the mixture and toss to cover well. Cover a large frying pan with olive oil and fry lamb shanks until browned from both sides.

Add the garlic and chopped onion to the pan and cook until lightly softened.

Place the lamb into Slow Cooker; add wine, stock, rosemary, pasta and bay leaves. Add carrots and peas to the dish.

Cover the dish and cook for 3-4 hours on HIGH temperature.

Before the serving stir in minced parsley and season with salt and pepper.

**Nutrition: Calories: 602 Fat: 9g Carbohydrates: 21g Protein: 60g**

## Spicy chicken with fennel stew

The long time infuses the chicken flavor and makes your lunch delicious and spicy!

**Prep time: 15 minutes Cooking time: 5 hours Servings: 4**

**INGREDIENTS:**

**Olive oil**

**Two fennel bulbs**

**Two chicken thighs**

**Two tablespoons flour (plain)**

**Four anchovies (chopped finely)**

**Three garlic cloves**

**One red chili (chopped)**

**Can diced tomatoes**

**Half cup white wine**

**Italian bread (to serve)**

**Fennel fronds (to garnish)**

DIRECTIONS:

Heat a skillet over medium temperature and add one tablespoon of olive oil. Add fennel and cook stirring until golden (for 6-8 minutes)

Transfer kennel to the Slow Cooker and heat the remaining olive oil in the same skillet.

Cut the chicken and toss in flour, so it will coat evenly. Fry for 6-7 minutes (until browned well). Add anchovy, garlic and chili to chicken and cook for another 2-3 minutes.

Add wine, wait until boil and then simmer for a couple minutes. Add tomatoes and transfer chicken to Slow Cooker.

Cover and cook on LOW for 5 hours.

To serve, cut the bread and garnish with fennels.

**Nutrition: Calories: 1536 Fat: 25g Carbohydrates: 18g Protein: 48g**

## French Farmhouse Chicken Soup

Perfect for a winter or fall day, when you need to warm with a bowl of hot soup.

**Prep time: 10 minutes Cooking time: 6 hours Servings: 4**

**INGREDIENTS:**

**2 tsp olive oil (extra virgin)**

**6 chicken eggs**

**2 carrots (diced)**

**2 celery stalks (trimmed and sliced)**

**One leek (thinly sliced)**

**1 fennel bulb (diced)**

**Chicken stock (salt-reduced)**

**3 thyme sprigs (fresh)**

**Half cup frozen peas**

**Four slices crusty bread (to serve)**

## DIRECTIONS:

Heat the olive oil in a non-stick skillet over medium heat.

Add chicken and fry for 5-7 minutes until browned from all sides. Transfer to the Slow Cooker. Cover the chicken with carrot, celery, fennel, leek, thyme and stock. Add salt and pepper to taste. Cover the lid of the Slow Cooker and cook for around 5 hours on LOW temperature.

When cooking time is almost over, add the peas (in the last 10-15 minutes).

Take the chicken off the soup and remove all the bones. Shred roughly and place back to soup. Sprinkle with fennel fronds and serve the soup with crusty bread.

**Nutrition: Calories: 850 Fat: 12g Carbohydrates: 64g Protein: 50g**

## Bean soup served with toasts

Warm and satisfying soup with beans and toasts to maintain your day!

**Prep time: 12 minutes Cooking time: 7 hours Servings: 4**

INGREDIENTS:

**One cup borlotti beans (dried)**

**One large brown onion (finely chopped)**

**1 tsp olive oil (extra virgin)**

**4 celery sticks**

**1large carrot**

**Finely chopped pancetta**

**3 garlic cloves**

**2tsp fresh rosemary (chopped)**

**1 red chili**

**2 cups chicken stock**

**2 cups water**

**Tuscan cabbage**

**4 slices grilled bread**

**1 tbsp. fresh basil**

### DIRECTIONS:

Place the beans in a large bowl and cover with cold water. Leave overnight to soak then drain. Put the beans in a saucepan and cover with cold water. Set the medium heat and wait until boil. Cook for around 10 minutes.

Preheat the olive oil in a non-stick skillet over medium heat.

Chop the onion, carrot, celery and pancetta and cook until soft (for 4-5 minutes). Add the garlic, chili and rosemary. Cook until aromatic.

Preheat the Slow Cooker and place in the onion mixture, stock, beans and water. Cover and boil on LOW for 6-7 hours.

Serve in small bowls with toast.

**Nutrition: Calories: 540 Fat: 9g Carbohydrates: 35g Protein: 20g**

## Chicken ragout with red wine

Just try and taste this! Perfect meal to get warm on a cold winter day!

**Prep time: 25 minutes Cooking time: 7 hours Servings: 6**

INGREDIENTS:

**1 tbsp olive oil (extra virgin)**

**1 chicken fillet**

**1red onion**

**2celery stalks**

**2 garlic cloves**

**1 carrot**

**Finely chopped pancetta**

**One cup red wine**

**One cup chicken stock**

**Barilla Fettuccine**

**Half cup pecorino**

**3 sprigs rosemary (fresh)**

**Steamed green beans**

**Chopped parsley (to serve)**

DIRECTIONS:

Dice all the vegetables finely.

Heat a frying pan with olive oil, set over medium heat.

Cook chicken for 5 minutes until it is browned. You can work in batches.

Add celery, onion, pancetta and carrot. Stir and cook for 8-9 minutes until the vegetables start to soften.

Add garlic and simmer for a minute to fragrant. Add wine, wait until boil and cook for 1-2 minutes.

Transfer the pan mixture to Slow Cooker and combine with rosemary, stock and tomato paste. Cook for 6 hours on LOW.

Shred chicken in Slow Cooker with two forks and cook for another 30 minutes. Add pasta to the chicken and combine well.

To serve sprinkle with pecorino, add parsley and beans.

**Nutrition: Calories: 745 Fat: 15g Carbohydrates: 43g Protein: 334g**

## Egg noodles with Red Beef

Fast, healthy and delicious lunch for you and your family!

**Prep time: 15 minutes Cooking time: 4-5 hours Servings: 4**

**INGREDIENTS:**

**2 tbsp. plain flour**

**Beef steak**

**1-2 tbsp. peanut oil**

**One cup chicken stock**

**Half cup dry sherry**

**4 tbsp. soy sauce**

**6 crushed cardamom pods**

**Sliced ginger (fresh)**

**1cinnamon stick**

**Half teaspoon fennel seeds**

**Egg noodles (to serve)**

**Coriander sprigs, to serve)**

DIRECTIONS:

In a large bowl, toss the beef with the flour to fully coat.

Take a large non-stick skillet and heat 2 teaspoons olive oil (over medium heat).

Separate the beef into three parts and cook in batches each one for 3-4 minutes. After ready, transfer the beef to slow cooker.

Cover the beef with sherry, stock, cardamom, ginger, anise star and fennel seeds. Sprinkle with soy sauce.

Cook on HIGH temperatures until tender beef (for 4-5 hours). Before serving top with coriander.

**Nutrition: Calories: 930 Fat: 19g Carbohydrates: 7g Protein: 45g**

## Autumn Pumpkin Soup

Get warm and eat a tasty autumn soup!

**Prep time: 30 minutes Cooking time: 4 hours Servings: 4-6**

INGREDIENTS:

**Half medium-sized butternut pumpkin**

**2-3 medium potatoes**

**Salt**

**Black pepper (cracked)**

**1-2 tsp mild curry powder**

**1 onion**

**One cup cream (full)**

**Chili powder to taste (optional)**

**2 cups vegetable stock**

DIRECTIONS:

Cut and peel the pumpkin, remove skin and seeds. Chop the potatoes and fine dice the onion.

Place the vegetables in the Slow Cooker. Add salt and pepper.

Cook for 4-6 hours on LOW temperatures until the pumpkin and potatoes are tender. When ready, wait until cool and stir with a food processor until smooth consistence. Stir in the chili powder and cream.

To serve, warm again a little bit.

**Nutrition: Calories: 355 Fat: 9g Carbohydrates: 5g Protein: 21g**

## Bone Broth in Slow Cooker

The perfect choice for a cold winter day!

**Prep time: 15 minutes Cooking time: 24 hours Servings: 6**

INGREDIENTS:

**Beef bones (you can gather a mix of knuckle, marrow and meat bones)**

**6 sprigs thyme**

**2tbsp apple cider vinegar**

**1 browned onion (halved)**

**2 quartered carrots**

**4 garlic cloves**

**One bay leaf**

**2 chopped stalks celery**

DIRECTIONS:

Preheat your oven 200 degrees (or 180, if your oven is fan-forced). Place your bone mix on a roasting tray and cook for 30-40 minutes. Place all the bones and fat in Slow Cooker.

Add the quartered carrots, garlic, halved onion and chopped celery. Pour the water to cover the ingredients.

Close the lid and simmer for 24 hours on LOW (you can add more water if some vaporize during the cooking time).

Take off and strain into a separate large bowl. Chill before serving.

**Nutrition: Calories: 293 Fat: 1g Carbohydrates: 5g Protein: 13g**

# Creamy vegetable curry with chickpea

Try to cook this during summer season!

**Prep time: 20 minutes Cooking time: 4 hours Servings: 6**

**INGREDIENTS:**

**2 tsp vegetable oil**

**2 tbsp. Madras curry paste**

**One can light coconut cream**

**1 red capsicum**

**1 small cauliflower (cut into florets)**

**One medium pumpkin (cut into small cubes)**

**3 chopped tomatoes**

**One cup green beans**

**Two cups chickpeas**

**1Lebanese cucumber**

**One cup plain Greek yogurt**

**4 bread slices**

DIRECTIONS:

Cut the capsicum, pumpkin and cucumber into small cubes, Chop the tomatoes, halve the beans, drain and rinse chickpeas.

Heat olive oil in a large saucepan over medium heat.

Add curry paste and stock. Wait until simmer and transfer to Slow Cooker. Add the pumpkin, capsicum and coconut cream to the Slow Cooker.

Cook on LOW temperature for 3 hours.

Add tomato and cauliflower. Cook for another 15 minutes. Cover with chickpeas and beans, prepare for 30 minutes.

To serve, combine coriander, cucumber and yogurt in a separate bowl. Serve with the bread and yogurt.

**Nutrition: Calories: 773 Fat: 20g Carbohydrates: 51g Protein: 20g**

# Lamb Chunks with Honey

Make your lunch warm and sweet!

**Prep time: 20 minutes Cooking time: 4 hours Servings: 4**

INGREDIENTS:

**Half cup soy sauce**

**3 tbsp honey**

**2garlic cloves**

**Black pepper**

**1 star anise**

**Fresh ginger**

**1 brown inion**

**1 tbsp vegetable oil**

**1 sliced orange**

**4 lamb shanks**

**1 red chili**

**1 tsp sesame oil**

**1 green onion**

**4 cups rice (steamed)**

**Halved baby pak choy**

DIRECTIONS:

In separate bowl, combine honey, soy sauce, garlic, ginger, black pepper and star anise. Put diced brown onion and carrots in Slow Cooker.

Add the sliced orange over the onion and carrot.

In a large frying pan heat the vegetable oil and cook lamb for 4-5 minutes on medium heat (or until browned all sides). Place to Slow Cooker.

Cover with the lid and prepare on HIGH temperatures for 4 hours).

Transfer lamb to a baking tray and cook in the oven for 14 minutes on 180 degrees. Meanwhile, add sesame oil, star anise to Slow Cooker. Cook for 15 minutes.

Serve lamb with pac choy and rice.

**Nutrition: Calories: 549 Fat: 10g Carbohydrates: 37g
Protein: 30g**

## Chickpea curry with vegetables

So delicious and spicy – your lunch will bring you new powers for your day!

**Prep time: 15 minutes Cooking time: 4 hours Servings: 4**

INGREDIENTS:

**1 tbsp vegetable oil**

**One brown onion (large)**

**2 garlic cloves**

**3 tsp ground cumin**

**2 tbsp curry powder**

**Half juiced lemon**

**One can diced tomatoes**

**One cup chickpeas**

**One large carrot**

**1 red capsicum**

**One cup cauliflower**

**Half cup mushrooms**

**4 small yellow squash**

**1,5 cup broccoli florets**

**To serve, jasmine rice, salt, natural yogurt**

DIRECTIONS:

Preheat vegetable oil in a large skillet (over medium heat). Add chopped onion, stir and cook for 3 minutes until soft. Add garlic, cumin and curry powder and cook until aromatic. Stir in mashed potatoes and simmer for 3-5 minutes.

Pour half-cup water, vegetables, chickpeas and 2 tablespoons lemon juice. Bring to boil. Spoon to the Slow Cooker and prepare on HIGH for 4-6 hours.

Serve with the rice and yogurt.

**Nutrition: Calories: 938 Fat: 7g Carbohydrates: 19g Protein: 15g**

# Soup with lentils and goat cheese

Set the work on pause for a bowl of hot soup!

**Prep time: 25 minutes Cooking time: 3 hours Servings: 4**

**INGREDIENTS:**

**One brown onion**

**2 celery sticks**

**1 swede**

**1 carrot**

**1 garlic clove**

**Half cup red lentils**

**One can diced tomatoes**

**2 cups vegetable stock**

**2 tbsp fresh chives**

**1baguette (sliced diagonally)**

**3 teaspoons ground cumin**

**Half cup goat cheese**

## DIRECTIONS:

Finely chop the onion, carrot, celery, swede, fresh chimes. Crush the garlic clove.

Place the vegetables along with lentils, stock, tomatoes and cumin in your Slow Cooker. Cover with the lid and cook until thick soup and tender vegetables (for 3 hours on HIGH temperature).

Preheat your grill and place the bread on the baking tray. Cook until golden for 2-3 minutes each side.

In a small bowl, combine the cheese with chimes and spread over the toasted bread. Serve the soup in a bowls with toast and cheese.

**Nutrition: Calories: 957 Fat: 9g Carbohydrates: 16g Protein: 27g**

## Ragout with Beef and Carrot

Healthy and satisfying dish for any occasion!

**Prep time: 15 minutes Cooking time: 4 hours Servings: 4**

INGREDIENTS:

**2tbsp plain flour**

**Gravy beef**

**3tbsp olive oil**

**2large onions (brown)**

**Half cup tomato paste**

**2 crushed garlic cloves**

**Half cup red wine**

**3large carrots**

**1cup Massel beef stock**

DIRECTIONS:

Cut beef into small cubes and place it into a wide dish with flour, salt and pepper. Coat the beef with flour mixture and remove the excess.

Heat one tablespoon olive oil in a large skillet and fry the beef cubes over medium heat. Place the beef into Slow Cooker.

Add onion to skillet, stir and cook for 4-6 minutes until soft. Add tomato paste and garlic. Simmer for one more minute.

Pour in wine and bring to boil slowly. Simmer until wine reduced or for 5 minutes. Pour sauce over beef and combine softly.

Cook on HIGH for 4 hours. Serve with the pasta.

**Nutrition: Calories: 731 Fat: 22g Carbohydrates: 10g Protein: 33g**

# Ham and pea soup foe Slow Cooker

Easy to make and very tasty – you should try this!

**Prep time: 15 minutes Cooking time: 7 hours Servings: 4**

## INGREDIENTS:

**One tablespoon olive oil**

**One brown onion (small)**

**2 sticks celery**

**2garlic cloves**

**One cup ham hock**

**5 large potatoes**

**One cup green peas (split)**

**3cups chicken stock-salt-reduced**

**Fresh parsley (to serve)**

## DIRECTIONS:

Chop small brown onion, rush garlic cloves and dice celery.

In large frying pan, heat the oil over medium-high temperature. Add onion and prepare, stirring, around three minutes.

Wait until the onion is soft, add celery, garlic, and diced potatoes. Stir and cook for three minutes, then transfer to Slow Cooker.

Add ham hock, stock and peas. Pour with 4-5 cups cold water. Cover the lid and cook on LOW mode for six hours.

Shred ham and return the dish in Slow Cooker for an hour. To serve, sprinkle with chopped parsley.

**Nutrition: Calories: 458 Fat: 16g Carbohydrates: 50g Protein: 32g**

# Summer Curry in Slow Cooker

Hot and spicy – just like the summer!

**Prep time: 10 minutes Cooking time: 8-9 hours Servings: 4**

INGREDIENTS:

**1 tbsp peanut oil**

**Beef steak**

**4 tbsp massamam curry paste**

**6 cardamom pods**

**1 medium brown onion (halved)**

**2 garlic cloves**

**1cinnamon stick**

**2large carrots**

**Steamed rice**

**1-2 cup coconut milk**

**6 large potatoes**

**2 tbsp. fish sauce**

**1 tbsp. palm sugar**

**1 tbsp. lime juice**

**Coriander leaves and peanuts (to serve)**

DIRECTIONS:

Trim the beef steak, chop into small cubes.

Place the beef cubes into the preheated large skillet with peanut oil. Cook until browned (for 5-6 minutes).

Transfer the meat to buttered Slow Cooker.

Heat the same pan again and add onion. Fry until softened, then add curry paste and garlic. Prepare until aromatic, and then transfer to Slow Cooker.

Cover with cinnamon, cardamom, potatoes, carrots, sugar and wish sauce. Pour in the coconut milk.

Cover the lid and leave to cook for 8 hours on LOW mode. Serve with rice and sprinkled peanuts.

**Nutrition: Calories: 534 Fat: 33g Carbohydrates: 45g Protein: 52g**

## Slow Cooker meatballs with rigatoni

Delicious and healthy lunch for busy people!

**Prep time: 20 minutes Cooking time: 7 hours Servings: 4**

INGREDIENTS:

**Pork and veal mince**

**1 tbsp. olive oil**

**Pecorino cheese (finely grated)**

**3 garlic gloves**

**1medium onion (brown)**

**2tbsp. parsley (fresh leaves)**

**2 celery stalks**

**One jar tomato paste**

**2 tbsp. sherry (dry)**

**2 tsp sugar**

**Rigatoni pasta**

**Pecorino cheese and baby rocket to serve**

DIRECTIONS:

Take a large bowl and combine cheese, parsley, mince, breadcrumbs and garlic in it. Using a tablespoon, roll small parts of the mixture and form into balls.

Heat the olive oil in a large skillet and add chopped onion and celery. Stir and cook for 3-5 minutes until softened.

Add sherry and cook for another 2 minutes (until reduced by half). Add tomato paste and sugar. Cover with six cups of cold water.

Place the meatballs into the Slow Cooker and pour in tomato mixture. Cook on LOW mode for 6 hours, and then add pasta. Stir well to combine. Cook for 45 minutes and season with pepper and salt.

Serve warm with rocket and cheese.

**Nutrition: Calories: 495 Fat: 19g Carbohydrates: 64g Protein: 51g**

# Cucumber Salad in Jar

Prep time: **10 minutes**

Servings: **4**

Ingredients:

- 1-pound chicken breast, boneless, skinless
- 1 teaspoon ground black pepper
- ½ teaspoon paprika
- ½ teaspoon ground coriander
- 1 tablespoon butter
- 1 cup spinach, chopped
- 1 cucumber, chopped
- 1 teaspoon chili flakes
- 1 teaspoon lemon juice
- 1 teaspoon avocado oil
- 1 cup lettuce, chopped
- 1 cup water for cooking

Directions:

1. **Rub the chicken breast with ground black pepper, paprika, and ground coriander.**
2. **Then place chicken breast in the cooker. Add water.**
3. **Close the lid and cook the chicken on High-pressure mode for 15 minutes.**
4. **Make a quick pressure release.**

5. Remove chicken breast from the cooker and chill it little. Meanwhile, in the mixing bowl combine together lettuce and spinach.
6. Sprinkle the greens with chili flakes, lemon juice, and avocado oil. Add cucumber and mix up the mixture.
7. Shred the chicken breast and mix it up with butter.
8. Then fill the serving jars with shredded chicken and add green salad mixture. Store the salad in the fridge.

Nutrition: **calories 174, fat 6.1, fiber 1, carbs 4, protein 25**

# Brie Cheese in Pastry

Prep time: **10 minutes**
Cooking time: **10 minutes**
Servings: **8**

Ingredients:

- 10 oz round brie cheese
- 10 sheets phyllo dough
- 1 tablespoon butter
- 1 teaspoon Erythritol

Directions:

1. **Place Brie cheese on phyllo pastry and sprinkle it with Erythritol. Add butter and wrap cheese carefully.**
2. **Place Bre cheese on the trivet of the cooker and lower the air fryer lid.**
3. **Cook the meal for 10 minutes. Then chill it for 3-5 minutes and cut into the servings.**

Nutrition: **calories 204, fat 11.1, fiber 0.6, carbs 7, protein 7.4**

# Pulled Beef

Prep time: **20 minutes**

Servings: **4**

Ingredients:

- 12 oz beef, boneless
- 1 cup of water
- ½ cup cream
- 1 teaspoon butter
- 1 teaspoon salt
- 4 oz Parmesan, grated
- 1 teaspoon tomato paste
- 1 teaspoon chili flakes
- 1 teaspoon turmeric
- 1 teaspoon dried cilantro

Directions:

1. **Pour water and cream in the cooker. Add beef and salt.**
2. **Close the lid and cook the meal on High-pressure mode for 30 minutes.**
3. **Then allow natural pressure release for 10 minutes.**
4. **Open the lid and shred the meat with the help of the fork.**
5. **Add butter, tomato paste, chili flakes, turmeric, and dried cilantro. Mix it up.**

6. Sprinkle the pulled meat with grated cheese and stir gently. Let the cheese melt.
7. Transfer the cooked pulled beef in the serving bowls.

Nutrition: **calories 280, fat 14.1, fiber 0.2, carbs 2.6, protein 35.3**

# Mushroom and Cheese Sandwich

Prep time: **10 minutes**

Cooking time: **6 minutes**

Servings: **2**

Ingredients:

- 2 Portobello mushroom hats
- 3 oz Cheddar cheese, sliced
- 1 tablespoon fresh cilantro, chopped
- ½ teaspoon ground black pepper
- 2 teaspoons butter
- 2 bacon slices

<u>Directions:</u>

1. **Remove the flesh from mushrooms. Then sprinkle the vegetables with chopped cilantro and ground black pepper.**
2. **Fill the mushroom hats with sliced bacon and cheese. Add butter.**
3. **Place the mushrooms in the Foodi cooker and lower the air fryer lid and cook mushroom hats for 6 minutes.**
4. **When the meal is cooked, transfer it on the serving plate immediately.**

Nutrition: **calories 307, fat 24.9, fiber 1.2, carbs 3.9, protein 17.7**

# Beans Pasta Bolognese

Prep time: **10 minutes**

Cooking time: **14 minutes**

Servings: **6**

Ingredients:

- 8 ounces black beans pasta
- 1 teaspoon olive oil
- 2 white onions
- 1 cup ground beef
- 3 tablespoons chives
- 1 teaspoon salt
- 4 cups chicken stock
- ½ cup tomato sauce
- 2 tablespoons soy sauce
- 1 teaspoon turmeric
- 1 teaspoon cilantro
- ½ tablespoon paprika

Directions:

1. **Peel the onions and slice it. Place the sliced onions in the pressure cooker.**
2. **Add ground beef, salt, turmeric, cilantro, and paprika.**
3. **Stir the mixture well and sauté it for 4 minutes. Stir it gently.**

4. Remove the mixture from the pressure cooker and add soy sauce, tomato sauce, and chives. Sauté the mixture for 3 minutes.
5. Add the black bean paste and chicken stock.
6. Add ground beef mixture and close the lid. Cook the dish on the instant mode to "Pressure" for 7 minutes.
7. When the dish is cooked, release the remaining pressure and open the lid. Mix up the dish and transfer it to serving plates.

Nutrition: **calories 99, fat 2.1, fiber 5.5, carbs 11.7, protein 10**

# Lettuce Chicken Salad

Prep time: **15 minutes**

<u>Cooking time</u>: **30 minutes**

Servings: **6**

Ingredients:

- 5 ounces romaine lettuce
- 3 medium tomatoes
- 2 cucumber
- 1 tablespoon olive oil
- 1 teaspoon cayenne pepper
- 1 pound chicken breast
- 1 teaspoon basil
- 1 tablespoon apple cider vinegar
- 1 teaspoon ground black pepper
- 3 ounces black olives
- 1 teaspoon salt
- ½ lemon

<u>Directions:</u>
1. **Sprinkle the chicken breast with the basil, salt, apple cider vinegar, and cayenne pepper, and stir it carefully.**
2. **Transfer the meat to the pressure cooker and close the lid. Set the pressure cooker mode to "Sear/Sauté," and cook for 30 minutes.**

3. Meanwhile, chop the lettuce roughly. Slice the olives and chop the cucumbers and tomatoes.
4. Combine the vegetables together in a mixing bowl. Sprinkle the dish with the olive oil. Squeeze the lemon juice.
5. When the chicken is cooked, remove it from the pressure cooker and let the meat rest briefly. Slice the chicken into medium pieces.
6. Add the sliced meat in the mixing bowl. Mix the salad using wooden spoons.

Nutrition: **calories 141, fat 8.1, fiber 2, carbs 8.82, protein 9**

# Spaghetti Bolognese

Prep time: **10 minutes**

Servings: **6**

Ingredients:

- 15 ounces spaghetti squash
- 2 cups of water
- 1 cup ground beef
- 1 teaspoon salt
- 1 tablespoon paprika
- 1 teaspoon sour cream
- ⅓ cup tomato paste
- 1 teaspoon thyme

Directions:

1. **Combine the ground beef, salt, paprika, sour cream, tomato paste, and thyme together in a mixing bowl. Blend the mixture well until smooth.**
2. **Place the mixture in the pressure cooker. Set the pressure cooker mode to "Sauté," and cook the mixture for 10 minutes, stirring frequently.**
3. **Remove the mixture from the pressure cooker. Pour water in the pressure cooker. Cut the spaghetti squash into four parts, and transfer it in the steamer insert.**

4. Close the pressure cooker lid and cook the spaghetti squash at the pressure cooker mode for 10 minutes.
5. Let the spaghetti squash rest briefly. Use one or two forks to remove the spaghetti squash strands.
6. Combine the mixture with the ground meat mixture. Mix up the dish and serve it warm.

Nutrition: **calories 109, fat 5.5, fiber 2, carbs 7.18, protein 9**

# Paprika Soup

Prep time: **10 minutes**

Servings: **8**

Ingredients:

- 2 white onions
- 1 teaspoon salt
- 2 tablespoons sour cream
- 5 cups chicken stock
- ½ cup cream
- 1 teaspoon paprika
- 2 sweet bell pepper
- 1 pound boneless thighs
- 4 carrots

Directions:

1. **Peel the onion and chop it. Peel the carrot and grate it.**
2. **Place the cream and chicken stock in the pressure cooker. Add thighs and salt.**
3. **Close the pressure cooker and cook the mixture on the "Sear/Sauté" mode for 25 minutes. Add the sour cream, chopped onion, and carrot.**
4. **Remove the seeds from the bell peppers and slice them. Add the sliced peppers in the pressure cooker mixture and close the lid.**

5. Cook for 20 minutes.
6. When the soup is cooked, remove it from the pressure cooker and sprinkle the dish with the paprika and serve immediately.

Nutrition: **calories 111, fat 3.7, fiber 4, carbs 15.98, protein 6**

# Lunch Cream Soup

Prep time: **10 minutes**

Cooking time: **3 hours**

Servings: **10**

Ingredients:

- 1 pound garlic clove
- 1 teaspoon salt
- 1 cup cream
- ½ cup almond milk
- 5 cups of water
- 1 teaspoon basil
- 1 teaspoon oregano
- ½ teaspoon lemon juice
- 6 oz turnip
- 1 teaspoon ground black pepper
- 1 tablespoon butter

Directions:

1. **Peel the garlic cloves and slice them.**
2. **Combine the cream, almond milk, and water together in a mixing bowl. Add basil, oregano, lemon juice, and ground black pepper.**
3. **Peel the turnips and chop them.**

4. Add the chopped turnips to the cream mixture. Place the cream mixture in the pressure cooker. Add the sliced garlic and butter.
5. Close the pressure cooker lid, and set the mode to "Slow cook". Cook the soup for 3 hours.
6. When all the ingredients of the soup are soft, remove it from the pressure cooker and blend using a blender until smooth.
7. Ladle the soup into the serving bowls.

Nutrition: **calories 101, fat 2.9, fiber 1.4, carbs 17.2, protein 3.3**

# Chicken Salad

Prep time: **15 minutes**

Cooking time: **35 minutes**

Servings: **6**

Ingredients:

- 1 cup walnuts
- ½ cup cranberries
- 1 pound chicken
- 1 cup plain yogurt

- 1 teaspoon salt
- 1 teaspoon cilantro
- ½ cup fresh dill
- 2 cups of water

Directions:

1. Sprinkle the chicken with salt and transfer it to the pressure cooker.
2. Add water and close the lid. Set the pressure cooker mode to "Sear/Sauté," and cook for 35 minutes.
3. Meanwhile, crush the walnuts and chop the cranberries. Place all the ingredients in a big mixing bowl.
4. Chop the fresh dill and combine it with the yogurt. Stir the mixture well until smooth. Add the cilantro and stir.
5. When the chicken is cooked, remove it from the pressure cooker and shred it. Add the shredded chicken to the salad mixture.
6. Sprinkle the dish with the yogurt mixture. Mix the salad carefully until combined. Serve the salad immediately.

Nutrition: **calories 287, fat 15.3 fiber 2.3, carbs 8, protein 30**

# Spicy Red Soup

Prep time: **15 minutes**

Servings: **6**

Ingredients:

- 1 pound tomatoes
- 4 cups beef stock
- 1 teaspoon thyme
- 1 teaspoon coriander
- 1 teaspoon cilantro
- 1 tablespoon ground black pepper
- ½ tablespoon red chili flakes
- 1 teaspoon turmeric
- 2 tablespoons sour cream
- 5 ounces Parmesan cheese
- 1 teaspoon salt
- 1 jalapeno pepper
- 2 yellow onions
- 4 ounces celery stalks
- 1 bay leaf
- ⅓ cup tomato paste

Directions:

1. **Wash the tomatoes and remove the skin from the vegetables.**

2. Chop the tomatoes. Combine the thyme, coriander, cilantro, ground black pepper, chili flakes, turmeric, and salt together in a mixing bowl.
3. Stir the mixture well. Place the beef stock and chopped tomatoes in the pressure cooker. Add spice mixture.
4. Remove the seeds from the jalapeno pepper and add it to the tomato mixture. Add bay leaf and close the lid.
5. Cook the dish on the "Sauté" mode for 15 minutes. Meanwhile, peel the onions. Chop the onions and celery stalks and add the vegetables to the tomato mixture.
6. Add the sour cream and close the lid. Cook for 20 minutes. Meanwhile, grate the Parmesan cheese.
7. When the soup is cooked, ladle it into the serving bowls. Sprinkle the dish with the grated cheese and serve it immediately.

Nutrition: **calories 144, fat 6.6, fiber 3.1, carbs 11.9, protein 11.6**

# Cheddar Soup

Prep time: **15 minutes**
Cooking time: **40 minutes**
Servings: **8**
Ingredients:

- 8 ounces broccoli
- ½ cup parsley
- 10 ounces beef brisket
- 1 teaspoon salt
- 1 tablespoon sour cream
- 7 cups of water
- 1 carrot
- 1 cup green beans
- 10 ounces cheddar cheese
- 1 teaspoon cilantro
- 1 teaspoon ground black pepper
- ¼ cup coriander leaves
- 1 teaspoon lemon juice

Directions:

1. **Place the broccoli, beef brisket, green beans, and salt in the pressure cooker.**
2. **Peel the carrot and chop it. Add the chopped carrot and water in the pressure cooker too. Close the lid and cook the dish on the "Pressure Cooker" mode for 30 minutes.**

3. Remove the pressure cooker vessel from the pressure cooker machine carefully. Discard the beef brisket and set aside. Blend the mixture until smooth.
4. Place the pressure cooker vessel into the pressure cooker machine again.
5. Add sour cream, cilantro, ground black pepper, and lemon juice. Chop the parsley and coriander leaves and add them to the soup.
6. Grate the cheddar cheese.
7. Sprinkle the mixture with the cheese and cook the soup for 10 minutes. When the cooking time ends, the cheese should be melted.
8. Mix the soup carefully until you get a smooth texture. Remove the soup from the pressure cooker and add beef brisket.
9. Ladle the soup into the serving bowls and serve.

**Nutrition:** calories 152, fat 8.9, fiber 2, carbs 7.15, protein 11

# Oregano Rolls

Prep time: **10 minutes**

Cooking time: **25 minutes**

Servings: **8**

Ingredients:

- 1 cup cauliflower rice, cooked
- 1 tablespoon curry
- 1 teaspoon salt
- ½ teaspoon tomato paste
- ¼ cup cream
- 1 cup chicken stock
- 1 teaspoon oregano
- 1 pound kale
- 1 teaspoon olive oil
- 1 yellow onion
- 3 tablespoons chives
- 1 tablespoon paprika
- ½ tablespoon ground black pepper
- 1 teaspoon garlic powder
- 1 egg
- 1 cup beef stock

Directions:

1. **Combine the cooked cauliflower rice and curry together in a mixing bowl.**

2. Beat the egg in the mixture. Peel the yellow onion and chop it.
3. Chop the chives and add the vegetables to a mixing bowl too. Sprinkle the dish with the salt, oregano, paprika, ground black pepper, and garlic powder.
4. Blend the mixture well using your hands until smooth.
5. Separate the kale into leaves.
6. Put the cauliflower rice mixture in the middle of every kale leave and roll them.
7. Combine the tomato paste, cream, chicken stock, olive oil, and beef stock together and stir the mixture. Transfer the kale rolls in the pressure cooker.
8. Add tomato paste mixture and close the lid. Set the pressure cooker mode to "Sauté," and cook for 25 minutes.
9. When the cooking time ends, open the lid and let the dish rest briefly.
10. Transfer the kale rolls in the serving plates, sprinkle it with the tomato sauce, and serve.

Nutrition: **calories 66, fat 2, fiber 2.3, carbs 9.9, protein 3.7**

# Coconut Spinach Casserole

Prep time: **15 minutes**

Cooking time: **25 minutes**

Servings: **6**

Ingredients:

- 2 cups spinach
- 1 cup cream
- 3 tablespoons coconut flour
- 1 teaspoon salt
- 8 ounces Parmesan cheese
- 2 onions
- 1 teaspoon oregano
- ½ teaspoon red chili flakes
- 1 cup green peas

Directions:

1. **Wash the spinach and chop it well. Transfer the chopped spinach into a mixing bowl.**
2. **Peel the onions and dice them.**
3. **Combine the salt, coconut flour, and chili flakes together in the separate bowl. Add oregano and cream. Whisk the mixture until smooth.**
4. **Grate the Parmesan cheese. Place the peas in the pressure cooker and sprinkle it with a small amount of the grated cheese to create the thin layer.**

5. Add the diced onion and sprinkle the dish with the cheese again. Add the chopped spinach and add all remaining cheese.
6. Pour the cream mixture and close the lid.
7. Set the pressure cooker mode to "Steam," and cook for 25 minutes.
8. When the cooking time ends, let it rest. Transfer the dish to a serving plate.

Nutrition: **calories 200, fat 11, fiber 3.6, carbs 12, protein 15**

# Stuffed Meatloaf

Prep time: **15 minutes**
Cooking time: **30 minutes**
Servings: **8**

Ingredients:

- 2 cups ground beef
- 3 eggs, boiled, peeled
- 1 tablespoon flax meal
- 1 teaspoon salt
- 1 teaspoon chili flakes
- 1 teaspoon ground coriander
- 1 tablespoon butter
- 1 cup water, for cooking

Directions:

1. **Place ground beef in the mixing bowl. Add flax meal and salt.**
2. **After this, add chili flakes and ground coriander. Mix up the ground beef mixture very carefully.**
3. **Pour water in Foodi Pressure cooker and insert trivet.**
4. **Take the loaf mold and spread it with butter generously. Place the ground beef mixture into the loaf mold and flatten well.**
5. **Place the boiled eggs inside the ground beef mixture.**

6. Flatten the ground beef mixture again to cover the eggs totally. Cover the mold with the foil and secure the edges.
7. Place it on the trivet and close the lid.
8. Cook the meal on the High-pressure mode for 30 minutes.
9. Then allow natural pressure release for 10 minutes. Chill the meatloaf well and then slice it.

Nutrition: **calories 105, fat 7.5, fiber 0.3, carbs 0.4, protein 8.8**

# Lunch Schnitzel

Prep time: **10 minutes**

Cooking time: **16 minutes**

Servings: **6**

Ingredients:

- 1 pound pork chops
- 1 teaspoon salt

- 1 teaspoon turmeric
- 2 eggs
- ¼ cup of coconut milk
- 1 teaspoon cilantro
- ½ cup coconut flour
- 1 teaspoon lemon juice
- 1 teaspoon ground black pepper

Directions:

1. **Beat the pork chops carefully. Combine the salt, turmeric, cilantro, and ground black pepper together and stir the mixture.**
2. **Rub the pork chops with the spice mixture. Sprinkle the meat with the lemon juice and leave it for 10 minutes to marinate.**
3. **Meanwhile, beat the eggs in a mixing bowl. Blend them with a whisk, then add the milk and stir. Dip the pork chops in the egg mixture.**
4. **Dip the pork chops in the flour. Add a splash of olive oil to the pressure cooker and preheat it using "Sauté."**
5. **Transfer the coated pork chops to the pressure cooker.**
6. **Cook the schnitzels for 8 minutes from each side. Let the meat rest and serve.**

Nutrition: **calories 258, fat 25.2, fiber 6.4, carbs 10.2, protein 22.2**

# Stuffed Mozzarella Caprese

Prep time: **15 minutes**

Servings: **6**

Ingredients:

- 13 oz chicken breast, skinless, boneless
- 1 tomato, sliced
- ½ cup fresh basil
- 5 oz Mozzarella, sliced
- ½ teaspoon salt
- 1 tablespoon butter
- 1 teaspoon paprika
- 1 tablespoon olive oil
- 1 teaspoon chili flakes
- ½ teaspoon turmeric
- 1 cup water, for cooking

Directions:

1. **Beat the chicken breast gently with the help of the smooth side of the kitchen hammer. Then make a longitudinal cut in the breast (to get the pocket).**
2. **Chop the fresh basil roughly. Rub the chicken breast with salt, paprika, chili flakes, and turmeric.**

3. Then fill it with sliced Mozzarella, butter, and chopped fresh basil. Brush the chicken breast with olive oil and wrap into the foil.
4. Pour water in the Foodi cooker and insert trivet.
5. Transfer the chicken breast on the trivet and close the lid. Cook the meal on High-pressure mode for 30 minutes.
6. After this, use quick pressure release and discard foil from the chicken. Slice it and transfer on the serving plates.

Nutrition: **calories 182, fat 11.2, fiber 0.3, carbs 1.3, protein 18.5**

# Veggie and Beef Lasagna

Prep time: **15 minutes**

Servings: **6**

Ingredients:

- 1 cup ground beef
- 1 cup tomato juice
- 9 ounces zucchini, sliced
- 1 tablespoon butter
- 1 teaspoon sour cream
- ½ cup half and half
- 10 ounces Parmesan cheese
- ½ cup cream cheese
- 1 white onion
- 1 teaspoon ground black pepper
- 1 teaspoon cilantro
- ½ teaspoon salt
- ½ cup beef stock

Directions:

1. **Combine the tomato juice, sour cream, half and half, beef stock and salt together in a mixing bowl. Stir the mixture well.**

2. Grate the Parmesan cheese and peel and slice the onion. Combine the ground beef with the ground black pepper and cilantro and stir the mixture.
3. Then add the butter in the pressure cooker and the ground beef mixture and cook it on "Sauté" mode until it is cooked (approximately 10 minutes), stirring frequently.
4. Remove the ground beef from the pressure cooker. Place the sliced zucchini in the pressure cooker and pour the tomato juice mixture to cover the zucchini.
5. Add the layer of the sliced onion, grated cheese, and ground beef mixture. Continue to make the layers until you use all the ingredients.
6. Close the lid, and set the manual mode for 25 minutes. When the dish is cooked, let it cool briefly and serve.

Nutrition: **calories 330, fat 24.1, fiber 1.1, carbs 8.2, protein 22.9**

# Meat Taco

Prep time: **10 minutes**

Servings: **6**

Ingredients:

- 1 pound ground pork
- ½ cup spinach
- ½ cup cilantro
- 1 tablespoon salt
- 1 teaspoon oregano
- 1 teaspoon cumin
- ½ teaspoon ground coriander
- 1 teaspoon ground black pepper
- 1 teaspoon cayenne pepper
- 1 tablespoon onion powder
- 2 cups chicken stock
- 1 tablespoon tomato paste
- 1 tablespoon olive oil

Directions:
1. **Wash the spinach and cilantro and chop them. Transfer the mixture to a mixing bowl.**
2. **Add ground pork and sprinkle the mixture with the salt, oregano, and cumin.**

3. Blend the mixture. Transfer the mixture to the pressure cooker and sprinkle it with the olive oil.
4. Sauté it for 10 minutes, stirring frequently.
5. Add the ground black pepper, onion powder, and tomato paste. Add chicken stock and blend well.
6. Cook the taco meat at the pressure cooker mode to "Pressure," and cook for 25 minutes.
7. When the taco meat is cooked, let it rest briefly and serve it with tortillas.

Nutrition: **calories 286, fat 19.1, fiber 1, carbs 5.53, protein 22**

# CONCLUSION

We have actually come to the end of this great and also bountiful Dishware Pot pressure cooker.

Did you enjoy trying these new as well as delicious dishes?

We truly want so, along with a lot more will certainly appear quickly.

To emphasize the restorations, constantly incorporated with our tasty and also healthy and balanced recipes of physical activity, this is a suggestions that we plan to supply because we consider it the most efficient mix.

A massive hug as well as we will certainly be back soon to keep you company with our recipes. See you rapidly.

Lightning Source UK Ltd.
Milton Keynes UK
UKHW050822170521
383851UK00002B/136